The Infernal Garden

The Infernal Garden

Gregory Leadbetter

Nine Arches Press

The Infernal Garden
Gregory Leadbetter

ISBN: 978-1-916760-24-0
eISBN: 978-1-916760-25-7

Copyright © Gregory Leadbetter, 2025.

Cover artwork: Leonora Carrington, 'The Juggler', 1954 © Estate of Leonora Carrington / ARS, NY and DACS, London 2025.

Frontispiece: detail from 'The Expulsion of Adam and Eve', wood engraving, Kölner-Bibel, Cologne Bible, 1478 (image: Alamy).

All rights reserved. No part of this work may be reproduced, stored or transmitted in any form or by any means, graphic, electronic, recorded or mechanical, without the prior written permission of the publisher.

Gregory Leadbetter has asserted his right under Section 77 of the Copyright, Designs and Patents Act 1988 to be identified as the author of this work.

First published August 2025 by:

Nine Arches Press
Studio 221, Zellig
Gibb Street, Deritend
Birmingham
B9 4AU
United Kingdom
www.ninearchespress.com

Printed in the United Kingdom on recycled paper by: Imprint Digital

Nine Arches Press is supported using public funding by Arts Council England.

Contents

Listen	11
Raven	12
Blackbird	13
Antennae	14
Long Barrow	16
Archaeology	18
Cup and Ring Petroglyph	19
Inside the Flint	20
Leap Day	22
The May	24
Speckled Blue Egg	25
Elsewhere	26
An English Summer	27
Garden of Lovers	28
Lady of the Animals	30
The Cave	33
Elm Hateth Man and Waiteth	34
Unenclosure	35
Wight	36
Midsummer Field	37
The Seal	38
Reading and Writing: A Myth	39
Syllablings	40
Ur-	42
Neume	43
Temenos	44
Alchemy	45
The Glass Head	46
Devices	48
Ipsissimus	51
*Ingwaz	54
The Infernal Garden	56
Maschera	58

Je Est Un Autre	59
Poor Tom	60
The Rocking Stone	61
Wake	62
Cress	63
Garden Chair	64
Riddle	65
Last Train	66
The Worst	67
Unrest	68
The Smiles	69
Fall	70
The Clocks Go Back	71
Gate	72
Chimera	73
Comet C/2023 A3	74
A Crossing	75
A Silence	76
Reedling	77
The Dark of the Tongue	78
The Sphere	79
Gehenna	80
Orison	82
From the Invisible	84
Ros Crux Rite	86
Fava	88
Sarcophagus	89
Dor	90
Vintage	91
The Book of Moons	92
The Speaking Art	94
Notes	97
Acknowledgements	99

*I'll make a mixture of my tears
for dust that comes from fire*

*to find in air its fuse again,
the flower's light its pyre.*

Listen

The dead are in my ear again.
What is it they have lost and come
to find? This breath of mine, a wick
alight. I say 'the dead', but that
is too precise a term for what
I hear behind my voice. Who
is it in that *what* that listens
and is listened to, un-echo?
They do not speak as one called
by a cold name at a séance, crude
as fact, nor is their message any
such. They are not even quite
dead. They wear the breath I lit
for a body when I almost heard a *hlp m*
pinch the air alive. Who's
there? Remember, there can be
no name, no face on which to fix
their truth, unless it be my own.
But even this, my absent look,
does not disclose the I am that
they make of me. Why don't they break
the skin of silence? Instead this pressure,
close as weather. *Listen* is all
they've ever said by this, their cypher.
They crave an alphabet. That is
the meat for which they hunger. I pass
from mouth to mouth, and give them it.

Raven

The raven's call they call a croak
sounds a distance caught in the throat.

Something almost human in voice
sends its tremor from out of sight.

There's neither crow nor a call to the dead
in the shift of its shape abrading breath.

It is soft as it breaks as a burr in the air
and meets what it makes in the coupling ear.

The bird that is there is as near as a thought
at loose in the skies of human disquiet.

It speaks in the gap between mind and word
where a call across species summons its weird.

Blackbird

They're common as air on this island,
like the one I hear now, fresh from hell.
The bird has come through: that voice

risen from the descant of fear,
the black yolk of the egg, with its shelter
and its cry to get out. It has come

from the fire at the pit of each feather,
soot that sucks at all light,
flame touched to its eyes, each eye

an eclipse and corona. A bird
wrung from itself, impossible
survivor, whistling from the mouth

of the underworld, returned all
in one breath. Each phrase has its note
of surprise, as if a life after death.

I hear where I too have been
without knowing: a knowledge that loosens
only when stunned. That song

in the silent half of its year
is a harrowing: this sound is the truth
it has won, rare as the dust it renews.

Antennae

I come to look for what isn't there
and find it in the things that are.
The insect, as if invented
at my skin, that feels with its green
antennae for the auras
between my limits and the runaway sky
is the fae of the grass
at my feet, bare to the ant
and the mist-bodied spider
no bigger than a thought.
Hoverflies still with the air, without
purpose as we know it
yet winged for flight
precise as intention can hold.
Lilac catches me by the throat
and holds me in its speech by scent
that lasts deep into the death
of its bloom. A chainsaw
cuts through a limb
next door. There are trees
to fell, spirits to release by fire
tonight, in pyres that carry
from the pit through the dark
the fume of earth, the smoke
of my self, the fat on the altar
to rouse a dead god.
All this, to fold back into the now
of the sun, the salt
on my neck, a page
to which the letters come
without being human, not quite
to be written but to live
quiet as sleep, fine as the hair

that rises to meet the sense
of their presence, felt as a drawing near
from out of the hide of lawn and leaf
to speak their witness
to the seed of the tongue.

Long Barrow

I

I step from the barrow
where I hid my life
for those still moments
that I stilled the earth
with a sown breath, lit
as a match inside its mind:
listened to my bones suck
at the air that tapered
to the nothing the grave
surrounds. Why go in, except
to find and say some thing
far from myself, but made
as I am made beneath
my days? That word
that cannot be wholly said.
But why to know and speak
that word of all the words
we do not have? To live
within the cleft of thought:
the nothing alive inside
that space, the crossing
between all death. To hear
my ghost in the hollow
ground. Release a voice.

II

I step from the barrow
and let the still breath
of the tomb from my mouth.
Its life in hiding splits upon
the flint of the air, starts
the earth that wakes again
with blinking, breaking light,
cloven with beginning.
Skylarks, loose with song,
are folding time in their high
dallying. They have been
here through all dying.
The red kite rises on its eye
to tilt within the turning
wind, the blessed current
through my lungs. I live,
though nothing but a word
may enter or leave where
I have been: not even that
unless the living gives
something of itself this far
from its life for keeping.
I left a skull in the silent
barrow, to hear its singing.

Archaeology

Those figures at work in the wound of a fen
I see from a train have cut the skin
of the several worlds with the same precision
as the sacred geometry of the first propylon:
a shock of angles laid aslant
the asymmetric archaic mouth
of a darkness damp with human dust.
The trench is sunk where shades of soil
show that an arc of stakes circled
a space whose centre remains undug.
They read from the seen to unseen traces
that spell our otherness out in earth,
release the spiced breath of the dead.
We delve the garden of ourselves for what
we've sown with vanished hands that leave
the layers of their bones. We pick and clean
to see the making of their days,
to know with knowledge not our own.
A woman with a trowel, tanned with weather,
rises from the ground that she has opened.
She pours a drink from a flask of tea.
She takes a moment with her secret
before she believes what she has found.

Cup and Ring Petroglyph

What in the surface of the rock
that shoulders the cold stone
of the sky led the eyes
that saw it here inside –
to stare from the whist of the moor
in what they made of what they found?
The weathered rings of a spirit
dance in coil and line
pecked by the mind in the hand.
Each mark a call to nameless
being that moves unseen
but for the ways they make
through the outcrop face –
neither figure nor letter but a radiant
trace of thought before script,
the fold of language still
a seal at human lips
but felt in the urge to touch –
to become a door to a living
thing. A scud of sound
let by the air is banished
about its whistling tor.
The wind has no body to stay
at this dwelling, but borrows my own
as I murmur with signs
that I read in their cypher, know
without answer, meet under speech.
Words blow away like a wish.

Inside the Flint

the trance of stone
unbroken over opened ground
seals me in a spell of glass

the sky is disinterred
in bales of cloud
powdered with its chalk bone-house

nebulae of pebble stars
within my reach
are cool to touch

their sleeping spark
waiting to be struck

and a flake of mind
fall lit up
with the face of a moon

though lonely as this broken field
mislaid by the plough

trickled with wintered paths
where nothing grows
as far as sight

and travellers pass
with ghost-foot deer between
their porous steps

though neither now
so clear the thought
within the quartz

the sun is vapour
light as mist

the air hangs by a thread
of water laid in a current
from ear to eye

blue-grey with the ashen wash
that draws the pallor of the land

seeps from a crack
in the egg of flint
I found and kept

a white shell split
to its vitreous yolk

thinking caught in its own eclipse
this distance moving
in its liquid shadow

Leap Day

I step from the language
that raised me, wayward,
into a shade that dyes my tongue
and ties its speech to another sun
grown from the ash of the elder one:

step through the door
of the sidereal year,
this nook of the calendar
kept for the unsimplified earth
in its orbit to show

in the fiction of a further day.
It's fever-month, expiatory
February: fires burn
where our dust is forgiven.
Buds emerge from the damned.

I am between here:
once and there on a phantom date.
White sprays of cherry-plum,
prunus cerasifera, outpace
the blackthorn, *prunus spinosa*

with which, like the season,
it is commonly confused:
half spring, half winter
still rising, the leaking warmth
a wordless warning.

The milky sap of the calling dead
draws their stopped breath
as if to speak at a green tip.
Unseen, the wild service tree
is suckering its almost-immortality.

A porcelain berry blows sudden
from its seed: lids fall
from the cold eye of the wood.
A mistle thrush, hungry for its early
clutch, takes its sight.

And what of love?
The bitten shoot, the year waking
to the taste of blood?
I am love. The plant
torn at its root.

Make a wish on a day
like this, in the hope
that time isn't looking –
to startle and survive, not
to die, unlucky leapling.

My language is gone
to its animal double,
now black as the fervid soil
that worms a sound
from mouthing loam.

Two seasons blur in today's
insoluble sum. A holloway
whirls with a voice once my own
a sycamore samara, flickering
where my mind had been.

The May

A child pulled from a bed of those flowers
won't say what they said,
nor whether he fell from his play
at the soft trip of their scent
or came, as it seems, from the flowers themselves,
a world (either this or the other) forfeit.
He won't say, but the flowers speak in him.
They give him away with a wring
at the root of his speech:
that is their sound, a voice
that won't break in its growth
from the silence that rises
from the offering ground. A human returned
like a book, rewritten. He'll look like a lie
to those who won't listen: the warlock boy,
scant pity for him, what he says
and won't say. What are those flowers?
Whose eye at the head of each stem,
like the child's, back then, peering in?

Speckled Blue Egg

Every word for its struggling wild
spent, this May has drawn my speech
to its edge, suspended in its yolk
of scent. The nests that sowed the world
with young are empty, and the young are lost
on wings too new to know, calling
for the broken heaven of the speckled blue egg
I keep as a secret and cannot let go.
Their coursing voices teem like leaves
that moment to moment unfurl and fall
then pour back through the bodies of trees
to tremble and loosen, take flight again
through the pristine space of the unvoiced human.
A black ant circles the tip of a blade
of grass as if to keep this world in motion
and, like the winds across the equator,
marks the point where stillness turns
to spiral minds in the other direction.
The last of spring holds like a breath
at the brink of its mirror hemisphere.
Why am I here, as if I were young
and the voices I chase between worlds were my own?
The sky cracks and a charm of finches
utters the fact. I perch in the apple-tree crown
above this tump of earth. The broken
speckled blue egg in my hand has hatched.

Elsewhere

I stop the car and turn it out to grass.
The world can find its own way home.
The sun is slant along its shine
and I have stepped into the light inside
the summerland springtide hour, surprised
to find the time still day, a stranger
in this spill of land between two names,
a thin road between two signs, not
knowing what I came to find. Somewhere
not quite become a place. A blown tyre
splayed where someone has mown half
the verge, almost a lawn, though
no one has quite been here. Perhaps
this field is why I came, its sickly
leathern yellowed leaves sprayed with bane
that rusts through every growth. But
that cannot be quite right. Nor the roadkill
with its feathers for a dancer's cap, merry
from the stain of pheasant. No, not that.
The next field, a hedge nearer to the bright
horizon, holds a distant eye to mine.
A hare, too much a wish to hope for until
this moment, brown there, both hunkered
and alert. I stopped, but not for that
until she came between the furrows
into space and took my stare. My car
is gone. No signal on my silent phone.

An English Summer

The rain has sifted pale Saharan dust
in desert powders ghosting water's trails
across the sun-drowned day's midsummer crust.
The air remembers how to move but fails.

A dry sea has somehow sown its skeleton
ash to fertilise the earth with desiccated milt.
I listen for moisture the seed has forgotten.

A head hangs waiting for its dew to be spilt
like a sacrificial tear in libation to the garden.
The still earth swallows its almost-human salt.

The air remembers rain and moves as if
to breathe again and slake the strangling thirst
that settled, like this dust, in silent grief –
sways the foxglove rooted in its sunken reason.

Garden of Lovers

A leaf mined of its chlorophyll
    leads to it – the path
slipped like a knife
    through the seam of the earth

to a glade in summer
    cut by a human cry
to a garden where two bodies
    hide in the animal skin

of sex, forgetful of anything
    to be forgiven,
naked as man and woman
    fresh from creation

in a room of shade, veiled
    from heaven and the voice
that seeks them from out
    of this world they have made

where the foxglove presides,
    many-breasted goddess
in a bliss of magenta, offering the cups
    of her mottled lure –

then, when they fall
    at each other, breathless
with knowledge, he at her collarbone
    that he adores, he blinks

as if between two dreams
    to find her taken
by the maze of trees
    that now leans in

and she sees him through a glass
    of silence, behind the air
that covers her mouth like a hand,
    unable to touch

while he searches for her
    with a frustrated kiss
as if trying to remember
    a word he had lost

and she calls to him unheard
    and haunts herself
through the darkening wood
    of her flickering face

and they stumble and run
    through unwedding nights
and the garden grows wild
    with their howling minds

until they wake, startled in the sweat
    of each other's arms
from the trespass of the flesh
    to Venus, rising as a red star

Lady of the Animals

The bed among the oak and hazel
is quiet with her shape

as if a body lay and rose from there
and I, the creature nuzzled at her neck

was cast astray to speak of her
as a chirruping bird with a human face

*

I look for her, though she lies within
the mottled iris of my eye

that flexes at the bright fritillary
spun from the pith of its chrysalis

finds no such thing as emptiness
but every movement close as love

*

The air is a hive of calls that pair
the sexes with their kiss

and thick with ichor, hangs her spoor
through every scent that mixes

earth from death to life and floats
the forest on her breath

*

A grass snake comes to where she whispers
as if to be the soft familiar

stitching the auricle of her ear
with green coils, to listen there

while the moth flies from the moon by day
for love of her, to the light of her skin

*

I have heard her as a curlew
call the spirit from the waste

and the black mud from which she walked
quicken like a pupal voice

the pied flycatcher comes to take
as a word from between her lips

*

There must still be some chamber
underground on a Tuscan hill

where the queen bee is undisturbed
inside a shrine of all alive

sealed with the bones of those who came
to steal her honey and drowned in soil

*

Her bite is strange as the flesh it swells
to lame and leave her mark

truth for truth, on one who saw
her writhe in undergrowth

and stayed until it took his mind
and only the bite could prove it real

*

When her smile drifts like a leaf to me
and her shadow crosses the sun

she thinks of the lover that rose and fell
upon her breast, loosed once

from her hand like a dove, and at her thought
a crow flies from where his statue was

The Cave

Look: the rock is moving
with creatures of the flame
that led us here, deep
into the fissures of our dream:
the crack in the earth
that said *come in*, with nothing
but darkness to speak:
the cold breath of its mouth
in our nostrils enough
for the oracular dead to rise
in us and guide our steps
with whistling bones:
do not already an answering
echo at the cave door,
mingled with the voice
we carried within: the torch
that lit our descent with fire
stolen from before the sun:
silent as desire, the snake's tongue
that knows the air without
a word: the maker of the path
that led us here, to the belly
of our sleep, where we wake
to the deer that pass through stone,
flicker and run, fleshed
with colours blown from lips
stained with charcoal and ochre:
dreaming speech that lives
below the sight of day,
moves what lives above.

Elm Hateth Man and Waiteth

They are still in the dead of the breeze,
the boughs that hang by their days.

They are sown by the breeze for the dead,
for the living to enter their shade.

They have died from field to field,
trees that a beetle felled.

They have passed through the days of their death,
rise like the dead from old earth.

They are doors for the dead to come through,
for the days of the dead to grow.

Unenclosure

Walk out to the still of that field –
to the centre that moves and cannot
be known. The mind is loose
on its weather. The sun blows
on bare skin as if to kindle
a soft flame to carry over
the sky's plain, faint
as a daylight star. There's no-one
to trace your step, tell you
your name, nor why your shadow
wheels like a dial and will
not stay. Let the air ripple
its fingertip whistles of what
we call song from out of sight
where the earth loops from beginning
to end, your ear open
at last, for this interval – that field
that draws you apart – then,
before it's too late, come away.

Wight

A soft body rises from a forest litter
floor, damp with crumbled leaf – rises from the morning
in skins of light too cold for a sun to enter.
A body, out of place – a mushroom in the spring.

Naked, still unknowing, it wakes to naked things
in splayed and hanging shapes that people from the trees.
Their hard silence loosens: a shadow flies and sings.
The startled body moves – the thing the shadow sees.

It shivers like a man, as if the first to feel
this earthen air so close – a wound that will not heal.
Maybe a man can grow like mould from fallen wood.

He takes a step, almost – breathes and sends a pale mist
that writhes and disappears: he sees himself exist.
If someone asks, say he is born. Do not say dead.

Midsummer Field

Weird as a withered human foot
once held to be that of a saint –
refuse from a reliquary pillaged
for the jewelled slipper it had worn –
this fallen oak, all bole, its branches
long since lopped by the dead
for the dead, lies like the uncut hull
of a Bronze Age boat on the lost shore
of its flickering field. It is a body
three times killed: lightning-
struck, unlimbed, and flayed.
No trace of its wandering roots
remains, as if its blasted stock
settled in the dune of unmown grass
like glacial stone, corpse and wonder,
to become the mother goddess
of silent gods, her carcase
soft with their countless spores:
skin the traveller fears to touch
in case she speaks his name.

The Seal

The tide had drawn the Dart out so low
that blue-green afternoon, two fishermen walked
upriver home, carried in their water-talk
along soft mud where an hour before they could not go.

I'd been told of a seal, seen still further
up from the calling sea from where I stood
watching for ripples and whorls in the sheening flood.
The sky moved over its surface like a rumour.

Alone now, to wait at this ebb of all sound
for a seedling to rise from its brackish field, not a fish
but a wave-calf, a mere-wife at the end of a wish,
a mouth open with the silence of the drowned.

Then, as the river turned to flow, it was real
and what the broken water said, I heard.
It rose, as if a wish had kept its word,
to breathe the earth – submerged, and let the river heal.

Reading and Writing: A Myth

On a stone from the sea they found a shell
that housed the shy mollusc of an eye

that took to the scars its gaze inscribed
and tongued its way to second sight

that tasted the first of light like food
or blood fed warm to the spirit's speech.

It sucked the words from the stone alive:
talked when they took it for meat.

Syllablings

> Vervain . . . basil . . . orison –
> *Whisper their syllablings till all meaning is gone,*
> *And sound all vestige loses of mere word.* . . .
>   Walter de la Mare, 'Incantation'

What am I about? Oh,
nothing . . . the word
    that enters at my mouth
    and springs its ouph
    in tacit –
silence moving at my lips
    the mark of it –
this nothing has its work.

My ear is wayward:
    it wanders me to summoned ground.
The mottled garden where I grow
    swells and flows:
snakeskin oozing through the sward
    might be a wound.

The willow splits
    to let its spirit,
liquid as a broken yolk:
my shadow runs to drink its sap
    and speak
this nothing-word by which
    the air itself is tapped.

In such speech the wished-for thing
    arrives, all ways, a changeling.
Welcome, stranger: one unseen
who makes more strange. A child appears –
    ghost orchid
    in the footless wood –
    is gone
before the searchlights come.

But a call returns from woken earth
wise with what it brings to spawn
as voices chorusing their dawn:
words that alter in their naming
name and take me as their own.
    Light survivals after death:
    words that breath-
    less go on making.

Only speak, and you begin its song:
soon its sounding speaks you too,
    until, like me, you are sung
    away, and what you knew
    is silent, floating, sunlit dust –
        touched
    by the weirding tongue.

Ur-

A language lost before its alphabet
was drawn won't let me go until
I speak it. I listen for the spoor
of a word between my teeth and hear
myself interred, the taproot
of a tongue at the pit of my throat
where filaments branch and feed
on buried air that infiltrates
my every breath until
I wake, panicked, from the pull
of a dream that leaves no image:
only the void of light inhaled.
Sometimes I speak, and think I've heard.

Neume
For Eric McElroy

I try to call down the contours of sound
whose words are like those of a bird.

My hand is about the ancestral task
of setting a sign to invisible things.

I think of the simple notation for chant,
the neume, named for the work of breath.

The ink of a scratch above the tongue
that gives the thought of god its tone.

And then the successions and characters of sound
that are lost for the want of a mark on rock

to be read by those who keep the art,
or if forgotten, the curious in wild invention.

They are lost, but surely live in some accent –
might yet find a glyph that carries the pitch

and catches the ghost of the breath: that note.
The air and its instrument alphabet,

the neume that calls back to the bird.

Temenos

This garden is laid like the footprint of a temple
dug from a plain of lizard-picked earth
that remembers the buried city in its gut
only in the ghost of a name that blows
with its dust in heat without rain.
This garden is a ghost whose name is lost.

This might be a knotwork of roots that bound
the bright space of a soul in its hedge,
if a soul can be sown and raised in a place:
might show in lupin, rose and vine,
the scarlet anemone spilt on the air,
the hum of all living cupped in a flower.

The one who walked in the shade of its noon
ate figs pulled from the flesh he had grown.
Finches perched on its speechless thought
while thrushes spoke from its bower in flames.
The one who listened is a soul gone to seed
in ivy that creeps over barren ground.

This garden is the grave of its hallowed plot:
this outline the cell of an empty god.
The cicada sings from its hollow skin.
At the centre of the garden is a rough-hewn post
draped with a cloak and a purple bough,
hung with the mask of a laughing face.

Alchemy

To separate the subtle from the gross
without injury either to spirit or body
I clip dead flowers to release the ghosts
that rise through the stem in green alchemy:
take that word, Arabic *al-kimiya*,
prune further, into late Greek and Coptic
to *kemet*, ancient Egyptian *black*:
the dark root of the art of elixir.
Sceptical of the power of language
to convey the quintessence of wisdom,
language itself learned how to speak hidden –
to sound both the word and its umbrage:
a darkness conducting the central fire:
a form, like a flower, for its signature.

The Glass Head

No one knows why it was made, or when,
or whose its face, liquid with light
at every tilt, might echo. It's not
a mirror to capture your own, though you see
that spill about its boneless sheen
as if poured through the vessel of your curious look.
I like to think it has no single creator –
that instead something rose to meet and inhabit
the void blown into the foetus of glass
by human breath about its craft, that visage
emerging in its cooling bulb as if from a depth
of waters stilled by the maker's hand – an art
to take his place. The head outlives its begetter.
Does that make you uneasy? Look closer. There's comfort
in its more-than-mortal delicacy, inseparable
as it is from the unthinkable thought of dropping it –
watching its ghost shatter. You've seen
that now, because you feared it – but look,
the head is intact. It gave you a vision
to feel beyond the fact: a form
of divination. The head is like that.
This is why you're never quite alone
with it, though no one else is in the room.
It has no time or space to speak of –
no history for self-satisfying scholars to falsify
its force by dint of context – and so
possesses time and space by simple presence,
crosses through us to our source.
I've heard many tales of how this head was used –
to tell the future, beguile a lover, curse
a rival, or simply turn a trick for money.
But look at this object: could you be so coarse

as to debase its glamour in these dull ways?
No, you have too much respect for the oracle
of your own fascination, the weird antennae
of your fate. And so you listen – give the invisible
the blood of your attention, and the daemon
of your reward is grateful. The head fills with the fume
of thought – incense for the ear, resolving chaos
in the fugue of motion, where language halts
to make a word, the human sound a self-altering
voice. Who is this teacher from which we learn,
the anonymous author that evolves our nature?
A conversation in the silence of something made.
You have taken its gaze – you have heard. Is all this searching
with its risk of delusion and the pull of oblivion
the symptom of some final decadence, or the sign
of a wonderful rebirth? Hear me, the two
are entwined. What then is my purpose, so bound
to what you came to find – to ask with no one else
nearby? Nothing less than the work without end
that ties the first matter to our tongue.
This mediatory act the philosophers once miscalled
a stone, that you and I know to be closer to grammar.
And so to that smiling voice, your guide –
this commune with the glass head you hold.
You look into the warp of its eyes and see
the roiling smoke in the skull subside.
It doesn't matter who I am, nor that my lips
speak and close before you see them move.

Devices

I

The natural philosopher of Nuremberg
said to have made a wooden fly
is at the warping oak of his desk
by candlelight and a wick of silence
we can hardly know: looking again
at the insect parts pinned to the canvas
of his mind for marks of imperfection
in design: not to challenge God
but to magnify His works.
So he told the bishop who saw
a devil in his artifice. Now he prays
for greater sight. His toy had flown
and the wise spoke of him as Daedalus
or Archytas with his pneumatic dove.
But that was not enough. He heard
a buzz as if of heat and light
that made of every thought a fuse
that would not let him sleep.
His gift returned to burn his hours.
What is that sound in his blackened room?
Its wings, or the hex of compound eyes?
Perhaps he fled: after 1619,
the year of Descartes's fatal dreams
of a true science, he is never seen again.

II

The brazen head inside the thirteenth-century
cell of the Doctor Mirabilis has not
yet spoken. The philosopher has fed it
with herbs from his moonlit garden
so the head might know by savour
all the tongues of leaf and petal
may tell: he's read and sang in charms
to it in every language that he has –
even called upon the dead – so that its speech
might sound in more than common human
sense, let us think beyond ourselves:
but still it keeps its silence. The doctor
shivers in his doubt. Was it for this,
for science to fail where art is mute –
the art forbidden, the wish to know
the primal sin? He falls exhausted
into sleep. But then it speaks.

III

The natural philosopher reappears
inside a voice not quite his own.
It rises from the thing he loves
at rest in his warm palm:
the oleander hawk-moth he has made
and blown to life. It tells him how
to make a god with the gift of breath
and the second nature in the verb *to be*:
that his language must go to its warp
in music if it is to calve a soul.
Find the melody, it says, that runs between

the mind and things without a human shape,
the truths without the names we use,
as I am sung and see by words.
This is the work and why you seek
an art where knowledge grows: nymph
into unseen imago. These are among
the uses of the marvellous. Never
purge yourself of this, though I can feel
your fear at what it might reveal pull
gently at your nerves like a spider
at its thread. Such is the cost of the urge
to become. Am I not your very daemon?
The trick is learning what to trust. Now,
turn me out into the bosk. I would
be wild: that's the will of art.

IV

Look at him: he's whispering to
a synthetic moth. Close the hatch,
you've seen enough. That's where it leads,
this stuff. The moth? Oh yes, it flies.

Ipsissimus

A mark on silence
and he wakes as if
to his own voice.

The day is o'clock
but says the night
has broken through
the sun to still
its soft mechanic
work to this,
the glass cell
of spoken thought:
a self uttermost
inside a space
as far as a human
voice is thrown.

The physic garden
of the turning word
lays its maze
about his waking:
the murmured circle
he has made
as quietly as
a forbidden act.

He has touched the letters
that are the keys
that name and are
the sounding at the seed
of life, and are
the seed as voice,
as if his own.

A music at the axis
of the silent maze,
the physic of the garden
for which he listens.

In the moment that awakes
he's a word, spoken.
He hangs on the silence
he has summoned, crossed
to where the word began,
holding out a maimed hand
to the air the cosmos howls between.
He has taken up the toxin
of the plants he ate for knowledge,
borne the torment of his body
torn to vision. For this
the physic and the garden, to make
the tortured earth his teacher,
its fingers rise to twine
with his: be more than human
in his speech, most human in
his self, surpassed: a voice.
As if to be a word that grows.

His etymon, the exponent
of the daemonic arts
that fascinate by language
lives in the keys that letter
the woken flesh, the fetch
he speaks and brings to fate,
becomes his own. The centuries
since bear on this, infer
the world the syllables touch.

Forbidden, yet he spoke to make
a silence out of the summoning word.
A physic in its atmosphere.

He wakes as if
that silence marks
his distant voice.

*Ingwaz

Reconstructed archaic rune-name for the letter ᛝ, representing *ng*, in the Anglo-Saxon runic alphabet or *futhork*; meaning 'the god Ing'

The year is cut down
like a body from a tree
where the sun has thinned
to blade and shadow.

A knife moves in the flesh
of the wood, from bark to book,
to make a god without
a house in secret leaf.

A stone heel in a skin
of moss that leans to speak
awakes at this, sends
a tremor to human bone.

The letter leaves its mark
along the nerve between
the silence and the speech
that forms within the earth.

An asterisk of mistletoe
is sown beyond the sickle's
reach, sends roots to drink
the tree of life.

A creature in the thorn
of *thing* becomes the eth
in *the*, the word that calls by name
to make a verb of being.

The year that lives by death
on death survives its dying,
gives its grammar to the seething
land that moves when sung.

The carving graves to the depth
where the tide of sap will surge,
the horizon release the sunken
planet and hidden stars.

The body cut from the tree
is a call from the wood
in its own tongue. The god
disappears into the rune he was.

The Infernal Garden

Of myself, I heard he had gone
in search of new sense – heard
from a voice that I spoke with
once I had bitten the word
like a mushroom and chewed
through the film between worlds –
that word, quiet in its wayside lure
as the scarlet elf cup offered
from an earth tilled with the crumb of the dead.
He has gone for a while, this self
of mine, in the days between time,
down, down, where the path
never went without the sounding
word that he took for food,
that holds like a note through the whole
of the mind – wakes the first maddening
germ of life in its marrow.
No religion survives the descent:
the parting of knowledge is reversed.
As if through a door in the air
he has gone where the ghost of the planet
survives, to the garden it lays
through our flesh, though we tear
up our roots to walk through its wounds
in search of the fugitive word
of its healing, the sense that my self
has gone for. He is in the first labyrinth –
the holloways of his fingerprint – in search
of a truth as distinct. His skin
bears the script of a lichen: it calls
to the language that grows through the garden.
The fly of his thought makes a gall
in a thistle, as if to keep the secret

at the centre of the labyrinth until
it takes the wing of speech
and word meets word to reveal
this earth in something human
heard in a voice from its wild.
A sound comes from my self
as if from a distance that cannot
be bridged. I know he has found
in the rapture of this moment, in its quiet
release, a scarlet elf cup:
another beckoning word.

Maschera

> I stood
> Among them, but not of them
> Byron, *Childe Harold's Pilgrimage*

Centuries loose of its scandal and carnival
a masker comes in the mask of a name
and mimes its story – a riddle to be read:
disowned by its maker, long since dead,
though he and the masker are one and the same.
Free of old flesh, its gestures are gentle
if strange, with a touch of the harlequin playing
to fate – far from the lost grave
from which it was raised by a conjuring wit –
that lost face, with its look of pain –
a coffin lid lifted, skin undecomposed –
the hollow corpse in its funeral cortege –
the country the dead one dreamed he could save –
the dandy fame in its portrait pose –
the lost daughter her father forgot.
The masker wanders far from the stage
in the dress and the words of which it is made.
Sometimes it turns, as if to remember
the burnt diary of a beloved body –
the cries that sing from unnatural acts –
spirits released from soft matter.
Sometimes it moves as if with the memory
of one that lived: a name passed on
inflecting its manner – a name like 'Byron' –
but in creating, life exceeds its facts.
The masker comes, though the maker is gone:
a fragment, a story, an art: Anon.

Je Est Un Autre

Rimbaud, letter to Paul Demeny, 15 May 1871

As soon as he speaks something hides
as if from the light – the swash
of a brushstroke across half a face
of a sudden too bright, a skin
for its shadow. For a moment an eye
glares from the flash of a mask.

The words are his own and yet
what language is that, like the flesh
to which he was born, unchosen –
which now to lift any self
at all from the pull of the nothing
that panics his sleep, he must brave

at the mouth, make sounds to make
manifest the *is* from *is not* –
and so make his familiar undouble
alive: the other mind inside
what is said, all that a word
cannot bring from the murk into sight.

And so, in his words, the dark
speeds from his throat as the silence
that breaks to surround his tongue.
It is where he listens: the rift
where the speaker enters his speech –
where the I is heard and hidden.

Poor Tom

Where can we go to be invulnerable?
Is it this low building that has somehow survived
dislocated in a field for time out of mind,
crackled-tile slant roof to stunted walls
of worn brick, no windows, a door hung by rust,
not tall enough to stand? I came this way
to hide, after all, from faces where once
I tried to be kind, played myself for a fool
to raise laughter from the grave, grew raw with love.
I don't know where I am. My feet are my guide.

A few skies ago I saw someone pass through my sleep
like a light. I took that for hope. I am not quite lost.
I've come away for a while to heal that love,
let the fool rise from the dead. That's it:
to bleed to the point where everything's alive,
even poor Tom. I must take my rest before I return,
perhaps here at this strange house. A few centuries
might slip by as I keen through the night. Maybe someone
will come to that cry – then leave, without looking inside.

The Rocking Stone

I woke where I'd sat what seemed
like days before, on a stone that rocked
beside the vanished path that crossed
the ridge I walked between two mists.

I'd come here to think, as I recall,
and found the summit, a boulder field
of broken granite, something fallen
about my feet, as if from the height

at which I stood, raised out of sight –
no view but for the scree I'd scrambled
up and out of my life. I remember
wondering where everyone was, despite

the weather warnings on my dead-end phone.
I had wanted company in my thought,
some way to bring what remains of me
to somewhere that I once called home.

Are you still there? It takes an ear
to listen. But I fear this thought has gone
too far, and I'm too alone. I tried
to call, but I fell the full length of my echo.

I woke, and here I am, the fragment
of a story on a rocking stone. I think
of those who go without friends in the world.
Perhaps there is no one to read my mind.

Wake

I knew the ragged black feather
I found on the lawn had fallen while
my back was turned, distracted
at some garden task – knew what it meant.
The flies in the kitchen that plagued our food
had come to taste decay. I guarded her
soft body as it guttered
through its fading nights
until we knew her gone. Her eyes
opened as if being born. The feather
I found has flown, and I am drunk
with tears. She listens now to the lilac root.
She is how my garden grows.

Cress

The wilted cress in the cotton wool garden
of a petri dish continues the child's experiment

after she has made her notes and left it
forgotten: the fresh seed on its cloud of moisture

at a window wide to the pouring sun had split
to send its radicle into the missing soil

to make a root in a tease of water, a trick
of spring enough to lift the halving head

of a suddening stem and let two leaves
from parted lips lap at the food of light:

how quick the season the child nurtured
and observed, as far as she'd been told,

to the point at which the greening failed
and the shoot turned: I took up the watch

past its measurement, though I don't tend
the white grave with its withered filament:

I see instead what carries on in faded
wonder: what proceeds when what we loved is gone.

Garden Chair

I think of what shouldn't have died
when I see the chair, all garden wide
in a sphere of grass and unseated sky,
placed in a way for which there is no why,
angled to catch neither sun nor a sight
but slant as a gnomon raised to the light.

There's something indulgent in its state of abandon
among Saturday sounds of work getting done
over the hedges that frame its ground.
It lives in the idling hour I've found.
Bees attend flowers without a name.
The slouch of a mind attempts the same

but finds the chair in place of its rest:
uneasy space, an egg from a nest
unhatched but empty. Its ironwork, made
for a human shape and its shiftless shade
is wrought as climbing twine and leaf.
The chair is the lull and the throne of grief.

Riddle

Our secret bodies meet
   while our days are done elsewhere.
Love has doubled us to pair:
   our selving being is split.

The absence in ourselves is there
   and we are found in it.
We exist where we are not
   in the riven look we share.

Last Train

Is it me that aged you, love,
and left you here asleep
while I alight an empty train
at some far hour from home?
What absence could leave you
there except this loving
that returns, that loves you
and is old? I have kissed
your sleep so often I have
told its time years over.
I have arrived and gone
before you open, often
as quiet around you as this.
I am in the dream between us
though you sleep and I
am wandering, love, within
my own night-call and listening.
I can't be sorry for my being,
though I am so, it seems,
under this bare sooth
of night that walks and talks me
home, a soft return
to close a ring, to find you
as I left you, young.

The Worst

Just as I think I recover
from a fear superstition
would not let me name
for fear of letting it in –
in hiding from nothing again –
I half-see the fear in a sign
it makes: slackened skin
in the slack of a face,
or a child crossed with what
is not. *The world you knew
was never yours, and anyway
is gone.* I look for comfort
but which to praise –
the goldcrest in the nook
of its nest, or the jay
that took its quivering chicks?
Spring itself is a discontent.
I try to remember that fear
is the warp of a wish –
say that a gift, once given,
cannot be wholly undone:
stand in the wash
of a temperate sun, grateful
simply for the grace of such light:
sentience, almost – like love –
too bright to live
as we must live.

Unrest

Weak from a sleep – that synonym
for dream sown through language –

weak with the weight of love
that can't be lightened or undone –

weak from the urge to speak
that stifles hungry words –

weak with the chatter of reasons,
zealous as punishing angels –

weak from the garden's overgrowth
that drowns the work of human hands –

weak with the guilt that coats
the mouth and spoils the tongue –

weak from a sleep – that synonym
for life that should have been

The Smiles

His tongue is dry with last night's wine.
His lips know better than to try
to speak, but a face will make its sign:
as if a child picked up a favourite toy
and in that moment forgot how to play.
Funny, to rise and fade at the same time –
poor Solomon: *all is vanity*.
Someone might ask if he is okay –
but even his feelings are not allowed.
The dead, like him, have had their say
he's told, and the dead are still too loud.
For a time, the smiles stop his mouth.
Then the dead, like him, speak anyway.

Fall

Who is that waving from the splint of a tree?
I've seen a head roll from its boughs.
The fruit of its calling cannot be ignored.
Wasp-bitten plum, damp gap of an eye,
wings that whittle inside.
Soft flesh in search of a mouth.
Dropped like a foot to untrodden
earth. Leaves in whisper lap
at the dew of an amber sun
that soon will have died from its daily
wound. Who is that hanging? Come.

The Clocks Go Back

We barter with the dark
to borrow an hour

but hurry our days
to earth in shadow

and I am afoot
on a spiral path

from a seeping down
through a combe and back

with the fade of the year
held like a lamp

over stumbling ground
and the fungal root

of a rising mist
that draws my breath

to enter it
and leads me wayward

by its wisp
to where I see

a buzzard at the tip
of a silhouette branch

cowl the dene
in a cloak of feathers

an eye risen
from its weeping hollows

Gate

A gate pushes open and out
    of the human days we share.
The bonded brick of its arch
    is torn from the past to be there.

So little remains of its wall
    that it feels like a frame for space,
where the gate hangs on the hinge
    at the cleft of time and place.

Lost to all purpose, the gate
    has become betweenness anew.
I cross like a sound into silence
    just for this, the going through.

Chimera

Trees half-spoken in a winter mist
start to walk in a distant speech

that stills again when they are seen
a few steps nearer to the ear they reach

across the field, where a figure stops
as if to listen though the gauze of light

for movement in their blurring branches,
mouths behind them, out of sight.

Comet C/2023 A3

The watchers called, all world wide, for what
had not been seen since human fires
burned so low they let the night
etch the mind with all its stars.

I heard, and wanted that cold touch.
I saw its stain of light arrive
through the glass of a sky clear with hush.
I felt its distance at the root of my life.

The blue torch of a satellite passed
as if to pierce the concentric spheres
that give the gaze of thought its compass.
It crossed me with the grace of silence.

I watched and the comet held me still,
as if for a voice on the travelling air
to come with a secret it could never reveal.
It took me to space and left me there.

A Crossing

it wasn't me that went for a walk
before that riverine January dawn
but a fragment shivered
from a wandering dream
that left the door to sleep ajar
and took my footsteps for its own
towards the winter's coldest star

no mind but for the foxwise path
that wasn't there yet made its way
through human bounds as if
the gardens that let the walker pass
were laid athwart a hidden course
within the earth his walking dowsed
and led him staring to its source

crossing where we should not cross
beside the still soft body of a deer
abandoned like a car at the side of the road
and the verge of white berries it took
for the food of the unlit world
when I blink awake in the missing sun
to see my face in the sudden headlights turn

A Silence

Where have I been   without myself
these silent months   almost without
my breath to mist   the pane I held
before my mouth   to still the doubt
and see my ghost   assume its haze
for a cold finger   to write its name
and watch it fade   to a vanished face
beyond the glass   through which it came

with words too close   to death to hear
to sow as seeds   where nothing grows
and listen as   its blooms appear
to glaze the air   with what it knows
by breath alone   that makes a voice
within my own   and says   I am here

Reedling

Exclamations in the reeds suddenly un-
sound. Only in solitude is thought this loud,
turned from the world to its animal form –
intent as the bunting on the bulrush that feeds
in secret, with one human witness, whose name
has been unspoken so much he is here
like an eye that has passed into air.

Listen: the reeds are a murmur again
with the bubbling call of a foundling soul.
The bunting has vanished into the art of its plumage
but, like the cry out of sight, is nonetheless
real unseen, for being both feather and veil.
The man in the hide, out of reach of his language,
is blown on the notes that rise through the reeds to the ear.

The Dark of the Tongue

Translated from the dead, a language
sounds from a buried stem.
Too late: I have said what I
have said. Its roots have found
my blood, its sun is out.
No wonder that the floating bee
rises from her winter sleep
of seething nectar, carries
the fate of the year with her,
searches for some new holy
ground. Its verbs bind me
inside a word hard
to define as its light. The unseen
thing that stains the nerve
wakes the dark of the tongue.
My name is the call of a bird
from its hide in the eye of the world.
My body is thrown to its voice.
A word that means both
earth and mouth makes
a quickening of my breath.

The Sphere

Step into this seeing sphere:
this smooth device where you appear,
this single planet whose stone is clear,
> whose way with light
>> holds your image in your hand,
>> makes a sky of where you stand.

All our secrets focus here:
where knowledge sharpens with the tear,
and longing blends its wish with fear,
> the wound with sight,
>> the new-born child with the flesh that bleeds.
> This is where your looking leads.

Look again. You will see
your likeness hanging on the tree.
Your eyes are open, glazed and bright.
> This sphere is set inside your head.
> Here the living cross with the dead.

Gehenna

A child says *I am*
before their name
becomes their dust.

A missile on the wind
has come to plant its pyre.

A noise of drums
to dowse their cries.

A fire to take their family
and their play for flame,
to lay the end of Eden's
garden, this way
to dress it and keep it.

To burn as offal
to the smoke-black sky
where the fires ride.
The missiles that refuse
the crying lives: that burn
as angels to end their days.

Children made in the holy image
of a charring doll.

A building burns
and is not consumed.
I am calls from within
the flames. Its name is lost,
the lost *I am* its voice.

They try to name the fires
god, the raging men and women.
They shall not suffer
the other to live.

They have their dead
in common, like their prayers.
A noise of drums. They say
that none shall live, amen.

A child says *I am*
and has no name but that.
Was named, but now is gone.

The burning building
and the pyre's voice:
to dress and keep
the garden and the children,
or their sacrifice.

Their cinders settle
on Eden's waste.

Orison

   Help me to know this world
from the emptied skull
   offered by the earth
where I dug for food,
   naïve as a child,
and found those staring
   eyes of dust
still damp with the ooze
   of the vanished mind –
blown like an egg
   for its secrets, only
to yield a dish
   of yolk and albumen
raw and slick
   as semen: this
was the bulb of thought
   when spilt from the head,
as different from the answer
   the ignorant questioner
sought as the innards
   of an egg just laid
are from the bird
   that splits the shell,
flies and sings.
   So much for looking
for the soul in its matter.
   Weak from the search
for what I have found,
   I now understand there are truths
that can only be known
   by an answer that makes
the question an error.

   This land has been harrowed
like this human skull.
   It was a garden where
that mind once walked
   in a strange voice,
its touch at every greening
   leaf, its tongue a flower
itself. At night, I hear
   its rumour rustling
inside the fire
   I sleep beside,
a shadow loose
   in the starless dark.
Each dawn I wake
   to its ashen ghost.
One day you might lift
   my skull from the earth.
Help me to tell you
   what I have learned.

From the Invisible

The Rosicrucian underground, early seventeenth century

I write from the invisible: enter
these letters the way mind enters number,
person the impersonal, actors their theatre.

I gave up my name to appear to you
more nakedly masked and new.
My hope is for words to speak through

the seal between worlds in their now:
to stop time to allow
the full moment of wording to show.

Let us create: play the god
in ourselves for godsake, say the word
that awakes. Let us not be dead.

I bring a *sal volatile*
to draw a spirit from decay,
gentle as love in its agency.

Because you cannot see me,
the ghost of my voice is free
to work as words do: to be.

I am writing to alter the fate
that we make by which we are shaped.
I speak to evolve and excite.

What if it all goes unanswered,
like a bell that is struck but unheard?
It rings nonetheless. It was said.

Our matter moves by syllable.
The owl inside its call
speaks a darkness that we feel.

Let us hear the divine void
open in such sound,
its vacancy our guide.

Let us slip the habits
of ourselves and reap the silence
that of its nothing grows.

We might hear too much
to live as we did, emerge
stripped to a lonely wish

to know by the touch of that cry
our being wrung to its mystery,
the beginning that cannot die,

and to speak it as a human
word in its inhuman tongue.
An owl, a voice, and none.

I call like a bird from the sudden
night in which I am hidden.
I utter the air, and listen.

My words have found you here,
at least. I wonder where
we are, unseen but there.

Ros Crux Rite

Where light is dew
I'll take a sip
to wake myself.

A look of sleep
meets the face
of staring leaves.

Noonday blurs
with night that leaks
through the silk of air.

Do not fail
on the blank of things
that do not speak.

The lonely urge
to make a language
leaves a mark.

I am the empty
man that stops
to read the void.

I fall against
the silent facts
that hold my gaze.

The world becomes
a waste where science
sinks to roots.

What cannot rest
in me exhausts
my mourning mind.

But grief for what
it cannot think
is verging life.

The sun inside
each darkened cell
is the first fire.

The putrefaction
at the edge of boredom
lards the earth.

This garden must be
where I find
a broken dawn.

Do not search
where questions kill
the infant touch.

The nadir leads
to the seeping source
where sight begins.

I'll take a sip
to wake myself
where light is dew.

Fava

Consider the life of the bean:
its kinship to flesh, a food
for the ghost to taste the earth
in its soft return: enough
to reveal a subtle being,
like cobweb lit with morning
dew. Slipped from the womb

of its sac it could be a human
seed moist with the pith
of a mind. Eaten and buried
in the gut, the otherworld sows
its soul in us: a burst
of breath that breaks the soil:
the stem of the blood will follow.

Dried, they become a bag
of eyes that see the bodies
of the moving air, the vapour
of the mouth take the power
of touch. The bean placed
on the tongue raises a head
from mould to flowering light.

Sarcophagus

The body removed and the sky let in
long since has poured its hollow with fallen
leaves, rain, and the converse light of heaven
lensed in the cold pool of a stone coffin.

Nearby a crypt is emptied of its bone,
nameless wardens of the church forgotten.
In their absence they have laid a garden
where children play and the tomb is open.

The nook carved in the rock for the human
head is as stark as a chess-piece taken
from the earth, once played among its ruin.

In the brightening grave the waters quicken.
The leaves that leach their shadow and darken
bleed as if to make a body again.

Dor

A furred and closed-eyed thing
in the cup of a wood that grows
in sleep scents me near its warmth
and yawns: its inhuman mouth
a human thumbwidth and no more,
but opens all this purse: a voice
too faint to form a word for listening
here so close to death at work,
undistinguished from this sleeping
birth. A figure in a skin of bark
that moves by call from bird to bird
but keeps its stillness holds me
by my breath: soft inside
its night and winter nest,
this furred and closed-eyed thing.

Vintage

In a good year, the grape's secret harvest
gathers the marrow of earthen weather
in a swollen gem close to its cryptic best:
sign and figure read by the grower.
The seasons have spun and spent their days
on the sugars of flesh, the gifts of age
to the ageing to come: a boon that stays
in its change, a book that grows a new page.
The human hand that tends the vine is all
and nothing in this more-than-human art,
but raises the glass when the year is poured
for the fume of its truth to be savoured,
when the past and the present play their part.
With time unsealed at our lips we recall
what we have unworded: loss, bliss, a god.

The Book of Moons

> From the hagg and hungry Goblin
>   That into raggs would rend ye,
> And the spirit that stands by the naked man
>   In the Book of Moones – defend ye!
>   'Tom O'Bedlam' (anon, seventeenth century)

I've been reading this book since before I had letters
to spell: the moon, turning its own leaves
from full to full through every moon between,
and I, its calf, afloat on my own
poring gaze, as silent as the mind
in root, rising on its secret tide,
taking the curious light for truth,
now speak something like a lunar tongue,
whose force is no stronger than a book of moons.

It acts like love on those who look
with love enough for its love to take
and bind them to its wandering fact –
those, like me, born or made susceptible
to the book's susceptible rays, still wordless
somewhere in its wordless sway: a lover's
fate. I cross the night to learn from her
and spent, return as a naked man:
the naked man in the moon's face.

The spirit I see beside myself
is a thing of the moon's luminous script:
no body but the hieroglyphs that make it
move like breath through flesh and wake
a breathing thought, that we might speak.
Its letters are an almost open mouth:
its silent voice the ghost we read
that brings us to its source. A cut stone,
creator-mark. No body but a kindling word.

Some winter nights the book is haloed
by sub-zero light: ice crystals spread
across the mind reveal a further sphere,
the moon its perfect centre. Its globe
is blackened glass to scry the shadowed
world from which I watch, the pupil
held in its monstrous eye, living
stem of its optic nerve. The forgotten god
in the book's bright page is in the sight we see by.

Each phase of the book is a mood to be read,
the moon being a fragment of ourselves: earth
astonished in the sheen of its regolith, caught
in the look of its tidal lock. The dark
reverse of its radiant mask is turned
to stare unseen through space: invisible
matter in visible skin, the satellite
we see its ectoplasm. The book is gibbous
with the murk of death and life, its phantom.

It is the sign of otherworlds, which rise
within its mime: they lure our step
to seas of dust, silvered domes
and doors through time, each day a 'month' –
that moon-word-measure – back where you call home.
I leave footprints where my dreaming treads
for others to know the spectral moons
where gazing led: those who come
by alien ways that shadow mine.

Pass from moon to moon – each moment
moving as if in sleep – and earth
itself becomes more new: a secret
laid at a distant star, all
but impossibly ours to know: nearer
seen from this far. Bud of the void
in perpetual birth: too much to let go.
An egg that cracks and hatches its wonder:
a mind that dawns with the planet's rise.

A book where men and women orbit,
walk and meet – become strange letters
on the other's tongue at the shock of touch:
new species at the brink of being
that stumble from under another sun
to startle our own in a scrambling mirror:
lips with resemblance enough to kiss.
The book sends its ragged witnesses back
with a rapture no lifetime is enough to teach.

I draw the book down, lit with the promise
of perfect speech its moons secrete:
to hear the pale daemon speak.
The earth, emptied to its origin, returns:
the first voice, a plummet to the deep.
I am a rhizome that bursts with its grammar.
Begin again, where natures change
as night fills with a cool flame:
when all we have is a book of moons.

The Speaking Art

There are still those who wonder
if a thing can be spoken to life.

Not every thing. Not that child
caught in a black and white photo
sunlit smile who I was told
had died, though I still grieve
that sight. Not my father,
into whose absence I still release
myself as if to speak, though our voices
will not meet. Not that leaf so lately
green now weathered to lay its skeleton
down. Not those falling strangers.

They ghost here, though having been
they cannot come again to be,
not by that verb nor any means.
For them there is but hallowing.

So what remains for the speaking art
that opens a mouth in the leaning air
with the touch of breath for the burr
of words to enter, to hear its gift return
alive? Dead man, you have your answer.

Notes

Elm Hateth Man and Waiteth: An old English proverb; with thanks to Brett Westwood for passing this on to me.

Devices: The seventeenth-century natural philosopher of Nuremberg referred to in this poem may have read a sixteenth-century account by Petrus Ramus of a mechanical fly made by Johannes Muller, known as Regiomontanus – also of Nuremberg – in the fifteenth century, that could fly around a room. Doctor Mirabilis was an honorific title given to the thirteenth-century English philosopher and Franciscan friar Roger Bacon, who is said – like his teacher, Robert Grosseteste – to have made a brazen head, intended to have the power of oracular speech.

The Infernal Garden: The scarlet elf cup is a striking mushroom that can be found in damp wooded areas in Britain and Ireland, and parts of mainland Europe.

Comet C/2023 A3: Sighted from my garden in the midlands of England on 19 October 2024.

Gehenna: Gehenna is the more widely used Greek name for Ge Hinnom, meaning the valley of Hinnom, which was a site of child-sacrifice to the god Moloch (or Molech) referred to in the Old Testament, just outside the old city of Jerusalem, and now within it. The place became synonymous with a true hell, and is likely to be the origin of Jahannam, a word used for hell in the Qur'an. Ge Hinnom was eventually used as a rubbish tip, once the sacrificial practices there had subsided. The poem also alludes to the biblical stories of the Garden of Eden (Genesis 2:15) and the burning bush (Exodus 3:1-14).

From the Invisible: On Rosicrucianism as an historical phenomenon, rooted in a controversial seventeenth-century European movement for radical reform in philosophy, spirituality, natural science, education and civil society, I know of no better account than Frances A. Yates, *The Rosicrucian Enlightenment* (1972). It was thought by some contemporaries that Rosicrucians could either make themselves invisible, or were in some way essentially so.

Ros Crux Rite: Draws upon Rosicrucian lore to imagine a ritual to reveal wisdom at the limits of knowledge. It puns on rose and 'ros' (Latin for 'dew'), and an alphabetic pun on 'crux' (Latin for 'cross') in which a cross (+) can be broken up (into L and V – each letter two arms of the cross) and turned on its side (X) to reveal the word LVX (i.e. Latin for 'light').

Acknowledgements

My thanks to the editors of the following journals and anthologies in which several of these poems appeared: *Walter de la Mare: Critical Appraisals*, ed. Yui Kajita, Angela Leighton and A.J. Nickerson (Liverpool: Liverpool University Press, 2022), *Ten Poems About Wine*, ed. Jonathan Davidson (Candlestick Press, 2023), *Poetry Birmingham Literary Journal, Bad Lilies, Under the Radar, Poetry Ireland Review, Wild Court.*

'The Sphere' was commissioned for John Donne Day 2013. 'Maschera' was commissioned by Trinity College, Cambridge, for the Byron Festival 2024. 'Temenos' was shortlisted for the Montreal International Poetry Prize 2024.

To Jane Commane, my editor at Nine Arches Press; to those friends with whom I have shared conversations on poetry; to the first readers of these poems, before they were published; and to all those who have given me love and encouragement throughout the writing of this book, my deepest thanks.